HUMAN ANGELS

365 Mantras for today

Every word is powerful.
The power of words creates my world.

© 2012 Human Angels
ISBN-13: 978-1494261641
ISBN-10: 1494261642

Text reviser: Ross Wilkins
wilkins.ross@rocketmail.com

To our joyous little angel Medora

How to use and enjoy your daily mantras

The *365 Mantras for today* are a collection of original sentences written by the authors. These mantras will lovingly guide you in your everyday life journey, bringing healing, joy, and a new Consciousness into your lives.

Each mantra that you make your own, will become a ray of light that you turn on within yourself until you, free from every darkness and every fear, become a shining beacon that spreads its light into the world. Words have great power, that is revived by the poignancy through which you express your intentions. Read and repeat these mantras with your heart, let them flow freely into the undercurrents of your heart and day after day you will heal your life.

These mantras are based on synchronicity: in fact, there is not a calendar that assigns to each day a specific sentence. It is up to you to choose your daily mantra, only guided by your Divine Self and by the energies that come into your life in the Here and Now. Simply by selecting a random number between 1 and 365 you can find your daily mantra. Read it, then read it again, let your soul internalize it; let the mantra work within you, in the depths of your Being. Sometimes during the day, you can recall it to memory and you can repeat it again.

Allow these mantras, these simple sentences, to become part of your daily life: when you are taking a shower, when you go shopping, when you are stopped at the traffic lights, or even when you are at work. Every moment and every place is sacred if you love and honor that moment and that place, by loving and accepting yourself.

Some of these mantras are here to purify and heal you; some others will help you in raising your energies. These mantras allow you to spontaneously choose your daily affirmation, you simply need to listen to your heart and your Divine Self will choose for you the mantra that you need in the Here and Now.

The Cosmic Intelligence acts through the Divine within ourselves with the purpose of leading our lives toward our own destiny, with a supernatural guidance of Love: this is how synchronicity works.
By choosing randomly, it may happen that you find the same mantra several times; it might also happen that you never choose some others. Those you often choose, show you which parts of yourself are in need of being cured or worked on.

In this way, day after day, you become able to heal your wounds and clear your life of every fear, every negative feeling, and all limiting thoughts. Until you become a Human Angel: a pure channel of Light through which the joyful and compassionate energy of Divine Love will flow free and unhindered.

These Mantras have already helped many people in finding their own path, bringing them light and inspiration.

Paul N.:"'What I resist, persists, What I accept, flows.' This book is full of little gems. We are constantly challenged by our egoistic minds, beliefs of dis-empowerment and victimhood, reading the daily mantras in the morning will have an impact on your life and return you to your real self, rediscover the Unconditional Love you have for yourself and then you'll be able to feel that for the people around you. Read and meditate on each mantra everyday for a year and just possibly you could transform your life."

Javier L.H.: "You don't know how with a few wise and honest words, you've helped a stranger (possibly millions of miles away from you) jumpstart a healing process. Thank you."

Paula W.: "I want to thank you for all that has changed for the better in my life since reading your words. Your healing light is so very bright."

Lightworker H.: *"Thank you for your daily affirmations. They are helping me a lot in difficult times."*

Aziz L.: *"I don't know who you are, but when I read what you write I remember that I'm a Human Angel."*

365
Mantras for today

1

I succeed in everything I do,
because I believe in myself.

2

I allow myself to heal.

3

Everyone I encounter in my life
is my mirror and my master.

4

I stop feeling guilty
when I disappoint the expectations
of those who would like me to be different.
I allow myself to be myself.

5

I stop living in the prison of ego
with feelings of guilt.
I have the courage to be happy.
I have the courage to be myself.

6

I love you because I love myself.
You love me because I love myself.
Self-love is always the key.

7

I never give up, because
I believe in my inner power.
I always have the power
to change my life, to solve my problems,
to convert my shadow into Light.

8

My destiny has not been written yet,
I do not resign myself to my fears.
I dare to live my dreams,
I dare to be great.

9

My old suffering is no longer
a good excuse to be resentful about my life.
My old suffering is now my strength
and my power.

10

I do not have any right
to judge anyone and to say
what is right and what is wrong to them.
I just honor the God everybody is.

11

Even if most of the time
I was not able to recognize them,
I thank my life for all the gifts
I have had, for all the blessings,
and for all the love I have received.

12

Whatever I did,
I do not judge myself
and nothing can change
my worthiness to be loved.

13

Yesterday I was,
tomorrow I will be,
but only Here and Now I Am.

14

I honor and bless my parents,
whatever they have done
I do not judge them.
I am thankful for the gift of Life
that I have received from them.

15

By being positive,
I attract positive things.
By radiating love, I attract love.
By being bright, I attract the light.

16

I never hide my true feelings.
I am not worried about others' judgment.
I love being myself.

17

I feel worthy of a wonderful life.
I feel worthy of happiness.
I feel worthy of love.
I feel worthy of all my dreams.

18

I respect myself
and I do not give anyone
the power to violate
the sacredness of my self-respect.

19

I am honest even against
my personal and material interests.
I live with Integrity, I always do
the right thing.

20

To love does not mean
that I am allowed to interfere
with the choices of the people I love.
I love and I allow them to be free.

21

I am kind and sweet.
I am patient and tolerant.
I am compassionate and helpful.
In my life, I express all the qualities
of my Divine Self.

22

I choose to respect
and honor everyone's Free Will,
starting with myself.

23

Even if I have been hurt,
now I open my heart again
to give and to receive love.
I feel protected, I feel sure,
I feel safe.

24

I recognize, trust and follow
the voice of my heart.

25

I am thankful for my health,
for my home, for my food.
I am thankful for all the things
that I have that other people do not have.

26

*I allow myself to receive Love
as it comes, in every form,
and not only in the way
I think that it should be given to me.*

27

*I look on
the optimistic side of life.
I convert difficulties into opportunities.*

28

*I release being judgmental
and through the wisdom of my heart,
I deeply understand the feelings,
thoughts and motivations of other people.*

29

I accept that those I love,
have different beliefs from mine
and I release my need
to force my truth onto them.
My love for others is always
respectful and careful.

30

I always speak
my truth openly and honestly
because I am not afraid
of judgment or rejection.

31

I manifest the pure Love
that I am in every thought,
word and action.

32

I release the belief
that I am not good enough.
I am fully confident
in my abilities to succeed.

33

I have the courage to say 'No'
when 'No' is my honest answer
and I do not feel guilty because of it.

34

I free my mind from every
thought of judgment,
criticism and condemnation
of myself and others.
I align my thoughts with
the highest vibrations of Love.

35

I believe in the power of 'I Am'.

36

*My life is too precious to be wasted
on doing things that I do not enjoy.
I have the courage to follow my passions.*

37

*I stop jumping to conclusions
and limiting myself
to seeing reality for what it is.
I value being aware, I choose
being present and attentive.*

38

Even when I meet someone
who gives me unpleasant feelings,
I am tolerant and patient.

39

I honor my life as the best life
my soul could choose
to release its karma.

40

Looking at myself
in the mirror, I see a genuine,
worthy and lovable person.

41

I stop thinking and worrying,
I relax and entrust all my choices
to the wise guidance of my Soul.

42

I honor, I respect
and I value myself.

43

I recognize all
the fruitless relationships
as dead branches in my life
and I have the courage to cut them down.
I renew my energies, I prepare myself
for a new bloom.

44

I overcome
my abandonment issues.
I have the courage to go on
being confident in life
and in my own capacity for love.

45

I am honest
about my feelings,
I base my relationships
on respect and integrity.

46

I dream of a wonderful world
in which everyone is awake.

47

I release the fear
of being rejected and losing love
if I am emotionally honest
and I experience the joy of loving
with an open, expanded heart.

48

Consciously using
the power of my Divine Nature,
I decree the end of my suffering
and the beginning of my new joyful life.

49

I activate the Power of Yes.
I say 'Yes' to life,
I say 'Yes' to my Divine Nature.

50

With love,
compassion and acceptance,
I leave others free to walk
on their own path
of awakening and salvation.

51

I let go of any limiting belief
that stands between myself
and the power of my Divine Nature.

52

I release my fear
that the people around me
will stop loving me and reject me,
if I freely express myself.

53

I change my focus
from my problems
to the problems of others
and to my mastery in helping them.

54

I detach myself from the role
I am playing in life, from my problems,
challenges and dramas and I am awoken
to the effortless freedom
of my Divine Nature.

55

The world is my reflection.
I clear my mirror and the reflection
becomes clean too.

56
Day by day,
I am becoming a better person.

57
I believe
in the healing power of Love.

58
In my life, love is always available
and endlessly present.

59
Today I take some time out for myself,
to do what I love to do.

60

With the eyes of the heart,
I look beyond appearances
and I see that everyone's True Self
is love and harmony.

61

I admit when I am wrong,
without trying to excuse my faults
and frailties. I live with integrity,
even when it hurts.

62

I feel compassion
for all living creatures.
My heart emanates Divine Love.

63

*I reset all
the illusory goals of my ego
and I align my life
with the purpose of my soul.*

64

*It does not matter
what emotional states
other people around me are in,
I keep quiet and radiate love.*

65

*I stop reacting in hurtful ways.
I do not act until I am able
to respond with love.*

66

*I have an unshakable faith
in the perfect and immediate solutions
to all my problems.*

67

*I release my belief
that I always have to fight
or struggle in order to achieve
something in my life.
I allow the natural abundance
of everything in the Universe
to flow freely into my life.*

68

*I am aware
of the creative power of my thoughts.
Because of this, I have only
positive thoughts.*

69

I send love
to all of the relationships
in my life that need help
and I let the power of love
work on them.

70

The space between myself
and the rest of the world
is not empty: it's full of the vibrating
energy of Love. I can feel it.

71

My heart is an endless spring
of bliss and joy.
I go there to refresh, purify
and make myself happy.

72

I am at peace with my past.
Now I am at peace with myself.

73

I am part
of one universal Mind
in one infinite ocean of energy.

74

I release the old.
I release all that does not serve
my higher purpose.

75

I trust myself.
I am able to make
wise and positive decisions.

76

I burn all my memories and suffering
in the sacred fire of forgiveness.
From the ashes of my past,
I am reborn.

77

By simply remembering who I Am,
I transform my fears into love.

78

In all the universe,
there is no one else exactly like me.
I am unique, I am Me.

79

Friend or foe,
everyone comes into my life for a reason.

80

I release unnecessary things
and unnecessary stress.
I stay focused only on
my spiritual path to enlightenment.

81

I recognize the signs that life shows me.
I rely on the perfect guidance
of synchronicity.

82

I stop doing
what I do not want to do
and what others want me to do.
I have the courage
to live a life true to myself.

83

I accept the flow of life.
I stop being dramatic when things
are out of my control.

84

I open my life
to the limitless potential of my spiritual gifts.

85

I remove negative energies
and presences by blessing
and sending them into the light.
I visualise the space
that is left being filled
with the healing energy
of love and compassion.

86

I breathe, I smile,
I simply follow my heart.

87

I do not react through the ego,
with anger and resentment.
I act through the heart,
with Love and Compassion.

88

I am a clear, open channel
and I let the power of the Source
work through me.

89

I trust my inner voice,
I rely on it,
I accept its wise guidance.

90

I stop being occupied
by wishing for what I do not have,
I am thankful for all that I have.

91

I stop trying to hold on
to what is known and I experience joy
for every new thing in my life.

92

What I resist, persists.
What I accept, flows.

93

Everything I desire is
abundantly available in the Uni-verse.
I give permission to the Uni-verse
to deliver to me all that I wish for.

94

In my life
everything is possible
in the name of Love, including miracles.

95

I unmask all that is false,
starting with the big lies
and the little lies I tell to myself.

96

I do not judge:
I practice Unconditional Love
and this is my way to the Oneness.

97

I am the Master of synchronicity.
I am always in the right place
at the right time, with the right people.

98

Before doing anything,
I make my intentions clear
and everything happens
as a perfect result of my clear intentions.

99

In my life,
everything always happens
in Divine Perfection.

100

I possess
Divine Intelligence and Free Will.
I love the wonderful being that I am.

101

I stop judging,
I feel the beauty and perfection
of everything around me.

102

I stop blaming others
for the problems in my life.
I take back my power to change.

103

Even if I am exhausted by my trials,
I welcome this new trail
as a blessed opportunity to finally
overcome my limits and my fears.

104

I cannot control my life,
I let it flow.

105

I look for the good in others,
I look for the good in myself.
I look for the God in others,
I look for the God in myself.

106

I observe
my emotions of anger
from my inner space of peace.

107

I follow the flow
and I am always where I need to be,
where it is perfect to be.

108

I respect everybody,
a lack of respect for others
is also a lack of respect for myself.

109

I live in Love and Light.
I spread joy and happiness.
I am the sunshine of my Life.

110

Everybody is meaningful in my life.
With humility, I always learn something
from everybody.

111

Everything in my life
is in divine order
and has been created that way
so I can learn from everything
that happens.

112

Every word is powerful
and I am careful of every word I say.
The power of words creates my world.

113

Thank you to everyone
who has been part of my life.
Thank you for being my mirror,
for being a co-creator of my own
masterpiece: my life.

114

I feel at peace
and supported by the Divine Presence
that is inside, outside and everywhere.

115

I am Love in action,
ready to help and support others
in respect to the Free Will of every soul.

116

I give my love to everyone,
'worthy' or 'unworthy', it doesn't matter.
I allow my love to flow
without conditions.

117

I feel unconditional
self-acceptance, I do not need
the approval of others to be confident.
I am fully satisfied with who I am.

118

I am not my thoughts.
I am the infinite and silent
space of Love within myself.

119

Because I love you so much,
I set you free.

120

I Am the Divine experiencing itself.

121

I am like a diamond,
pure in my intentions.
I am like a sword,
straight in my actions.
I am like a flower,
beautiful and radiant.
Everyone, through me,
can see the Grace of God.

122

I do not have expectations:
the best things in life
are always unexpected.

123

I clear my cellular memory
from the destructiveness of my repressed
emotions, from the poison
of unexpressed resentment and anger.
I heal my body and my life
through the power of forgiveness.

124

Everybody is doing
the best they can with what they have.
Including myself.

125

I feel all the love that surrounds me.
I feel it and my sadness
instantly goes away.

126

With the healing power
of forgiveness, I overcome
every mistake I have ever made.
With my compassionate heart,
I forgive myself.

127

I cannot hurt you
without hurting myself.
I cannot love you
without loving myself.

128

I am successful.
I achieve my goals effortlessly
because my positive motivation
drives me towards my goals.

129

I am the Void filled to the brim
and overflowing with Love.

130

I stop complaining because
I do not have enough love in my life.
Now I can finally feel that Life
is Love itself.

131

Because I Am,
everything Is.

132

Knowing myself, I know God.
Loving myself, I love God.

133

I release
my inherited programming
that I will disappoint my family
if I do not do
what they have planned for me.
I walk freely along my own path.

134

I am Love, all is Love:
everything beyond Love is illusion.

135

I remember my Divine Nature
and, as in a mirror, I recognize
that Divinity is everywhere.

136

I take a breath,
I relax my body, I feel my heart:
I am a precious, wonderful,
unique and unrepeatable
miracle of Love.

137

I allow myself to feel fear,
because I have the courage
and the greatness to overcome it.

138

Yes.
I say an unconditional
yes to life and everything
spontaneously happens.

139

I feel time as
the continuous, uninterrupted
flow of Love in my life.

140

I am connected to the All.
The All is connected to me.
Love is the only cause and aim
of this connection.

141

I stop waiting. I stop delaying.
Here and Now I Am.

142

I stop thinking: I cannot do it.
I only think: everything is possible for me.

143

Today I celebrate my life,
smiling, singing, dancing
and keeping my mind silent.

144

I stay my course in any wind,
because faith is my rudder.

145

My best way of solving problems,
it is to call them opportunities
and let things happen.

146

I give unconditionally
with open hands and with joy in my heart.
This is how I live my Divine Nature.

147

I take my life as it comes.
Everything happens in Divine Perfection
beyond the control of my ego.

148

Judgment is the way
I separate myself from the Oneness.
Unconditional acceptance is the way
I rejoin the Oneness.

149

I am One with Mother Earth
and Mother Earth is One with me.
Honoring myself, I honor the planet.
Healing myself, I heal the planet.

150

Even in my darkest moments,
even if I cannot see it, everything
is always perfect.

151

I experience who I am not,
in order to remember
who I Am.

152

I stop feeling miserable
because someone else is unhappy.
Only when I am no longer miserable
can I make other people happy too.

153

I recognize others as myself.
I love everyone as another me.

154

I am not my anger,
my fears and my attachments,
I am my highest potential.
I am the Bliss, the Love
and the Compassion.

155

*I am not here to live
the little life of my ego,
I am here to fulfil
the purpose of my soul.*

156

*I stop waiting for love,
because now I am in love
with myself and my whole life.*

157

*I allow myself to be happy,
I allow myself to give
and receive Love,
I allow myself to Live.*

158

The joy of Loving is all I have.
It's all I want to have.

159

I surrender to my Divine Self.
I am One with the power of the Source,
I am Master and Healer
of myself.

160

My inner darkness is an illusion
that disappears with the Light.
My fear is an illusion
that disappears with Love.
My ego is an illusion
that disappears into the Oneness.

161

Thanks to my past I am what I am.
I bless and I honor my past.
But now I let it go in order
to express my highest potential.

162

Judging others,
I give power to the mind.
Accepting others, I give power to Love.

163

I let my pure light shine
through the mirror of my life
and everything, as a reflection
of my Inner Light, comes to me
in beauty and happiness.

164

My mind is stillness.
I stop thinking, I stop seeking.
The present moment is my fulfilment.

165

I bless my life journey.
With my heart I embrace all my Life,
All that it Is and the All that I Am.

166

Feeling with my ego,
I feel judgment and fear,
feeling with my heart I feel
Unconditional Love and Compassion.

167

My breath is my prayer,
my life is my temple.
I am a sacred part
of a sacred Whole.

168

I recognize my life
as my perfect creation.
Through the mirror of my life
I see my inner beauty.

169

In every moment of my life,
I discover its gift of Awareness.

170

*I am happy not
because of something,
I am happy because I Am.*

171

*I recognize my Divine Nature.
I recognize Divinity
in everyone and everywhere.*

172

*I stop believing I have limits,
I leave my Higher Self free
to create my Life in Love,
Beauty and Happiness.*

173

I'm not here to judge,
I'm here to Love.

174

I am light become matter.
I am love become matter.
Remembering who I Am,
I return to my true nature
of Light and Love.

175

Nobody is better than me.
Nobody is worse than me.
In the Oneness, everybody is me.

176

I breathe with my heart.
I breathe in Love, I breathe out Love.
I am Love.

177

I am free to be what I feel
and what I want to be.

178

I am careful of the little things.
The wonder of the little things
teaches me of the perfection
of the whole Uni-verse.

179

I stop seeking happiness.
I accept myself for who I am,
I accept my life for what it is
and happiness spontaneously comes.

180

I look at my life
through the eyes of the Heart.
I do not feel separated anymore,
I am One with what I am looking at.

181

My Life always happens Here and Now.

182

I have faith:
everything will be all right.
My faith is stronger than my destiny.
My destiny is driven by my faith.

183

My fear of Loving is gone.
I Love to Love. I Love to be Loved.

184

I overcome the fear of losing.
I overcome the fear of changing.
I let go of what is going.
I allow what is coming.

185

I do not expect others to change.
They are simply my mirror.
I change myself and the rest
spontaneously comes.

186

I honor my journey:
every single fear, every single pain
is now a gift of Awareness to share.

187

My mind is stillness.
My heart is peace.
I am timeless Awareness.

188

*Other people's judgment has
no power over me.
I am totally free to be who I am.*

189

*I deserve the best and I attract
only good things into my life.*

190

I am a pure mirror of Love.

191

I love myself in the present moment.

192

Every time I fall,
I have the faith and the strength
to get up stronger than before.

193

I have no fear of my darkness.
My darkness does not exist,
it is only an illusion created by my mind.
I am never-ending Light.

194

My happiness is not an expectation
for a future that never comes.
Happiness is what I feel
at the present moment.

195

I attract only positive situations
and positive people
as a reflection of who I Am.

196

My life belongs only to me.
I let go of all the expectations
that others have of me.
My life doesn't belong to anybody,
except to me and to Life itself.

197

God is not a concept.
God is not a person,
living somewhere in the sky.
God is the feeling of joy
that I am experiencing right now.

198

Judgment and a sense of guilt
are how I sabotage myself.
Unconditional Love is how I realize myself
and the highest potential of myself.

199

I always have a good reason
to be thankful to life,
I always have a good reason
to smile.

200

In my life,
the most important changes
are not driven by anger.
They are driven by the consciousness
of Love.

201

I don't fear my fears,
I simply spread my wings
and fly into the skies of Perfection.

202

Sometimes what
I think is good becomes bad,
what I think is bad becomes good.
Things simply happen:
I keep myself out of judgment,
I keep myself out of suffering.

203

I am lovable. I am loved,
I am love.

204

I clear my mind and my thoughts
and I open my life to Wonder:
nothing happens unless at first
I think about it.

205

I trust myself.
I succeed in everything I do.
I succeed in Life without effort.

206

I accept my body and its defects.
I accept my character and its weaknesses.
I love myself as a perfect part
of a perfect Whole.

207

I give myself permission
to enjoy the present moment.

208

I let go of everyone
who reminds me of my negative energies.
I thank, I bless and I let them go.

209

I am as unfaltering
as a rock in the ocean.
I am as flexible
as a tree in the wind.
I am as pure and shapeless
as water, finding its way
through every crevice.

210

*I love the world
as a reflection of the Love
that I have for myself.*

211

*I totally allow myself
to feel every emotion, whatever it is
and I observe it from my inner space
of love and silence.*

212

*I stop beating myself up
for the mistakes I have made.
I accept that the greatest lessons
I have learned in my life
come from my mistakes.*

213

I do not give anyone
the power to spoil my joy of living.

214

In my life journey,
I do not care about my destination.
I honor and bless every step I take,
every moment in which I share
my happiness for being on the way:
I Am Life.

215

My Divine Feminine
and my Divine Masculine are
in true balance and harmony
within and without myself.

216

Love is my wisdom. Love is my strength.
Love is the source of my power.

217

I freely create the life I love to live.

218

I am the only one in my family
who can stop inherited patterns,
through the freedom of my awareness.

219

I am ready to be and to give
the best of myself.

220

I accept
and embrace myself
as I am right now.

221

I admit when I am suffering,
I admit when I feel fear.
I always have the courage
to be myself.

222

I always do the right thing
because I am honest
with myself.

223

I allow myself
to feel worthy of the love
I receive.

224

I do not give anyone
the power to make me feel guilty
for my own free choices.

225

I am faithful to my partner,
I am loyal to my friends.
I build healthy, pleasurable
and harmonious relationships.

226

Where my ego ends,
my Divine Self begins.

227

I liberate the power and the courage
that have been hidden inside myself.

228

I do not depend on others' approval
to accept and value myself.

229

I release my past
and my judgment of it.

230

I send love and healing energy
to all parts of myself
that I want to change.

231

I stop judging
and condemning myself
for what I have done
and for what I have not done.

232

I deeply listen
to the people around me.
Even when I am not in the mood,
I am able to give them
the attention they deserve.

233

I share the Divine
with everyone who comes
into my life.

234

I see myself as God sees me,
I care for myself as God cares for me,
I love myself as God loves me.

235

I am protected and divinely inspired
in every step I take on my path
of awakening.

236

I radiate peacefulness,
I am a channel of divine peace.

237

I let go of the belief
that life is hard and I surrender
to the loving flow of life.

238

I am not responsible
for others' actions and choices
but I am responsible for accepting them
with Unconditional Love.

239
I feed my relationships with love everyday.

240
I release my need to prove my superiority:
true greatness belongs to humble people.

241
I welcome this day with a smile.
Every day is a new, meaningful step
on my life journey.

242
My heart is a sacred temple of Love.

243

*I raise the energies
of the people around me:
my presence radiates
Unconditional Love and inner peace.*

244

*I accept everything
that happens as a manifestation
of the Divine Perfection.*

245

*I overcome
my victim mentality,
I step into the power of
my spiritual mastery.*

246

*I do not allow my past
to affect my future.*

247

*Every person,
every situation in my life
is the manifestation of the One Truth.*

248

I am ready for Love.

249

I do not hope, I believe.

250

I affirm what
I really want, then I wait.
The Universe will provide it
in very unpredictable ways .

251

"Thanks" is a simple word
with a huge power.
With a little "thanks"
I make other people feel good.

252

I do not hurt anyone with my words.
With my words I encourage, inspire
and heal.

253

I am fully satisfied with my life.
All that I have is all that I want.

254

I allow myself to be loved.
I allow love to come into my life right now.

255

With compassion, I heal the wounds
of myself and others.

256

I seek happiness for others.
This is how I make myself happier.

257

I accept
when someone leaves my life
as a result of the accomplishment
of our soul contract.

258

I am careful
with whom I spend my time.
I surround myself only with those
who encourage and uplift me.

259

I give myself permission to feel
what I am feeling right now
without judging myself
because of my feelings.

260

*I celebrate my friends
as a gift in my life.*

261

*My potential future is present now
within myself, ready to come into my life.
I welcome it.*

262

*I do not allow fears and doubts
to poison the purity of my Love.*

263

I have the strength to face
every challenge in my life.

264

I stop feeling sad,
no matter what the reason:
I enjoy life in the present moment.

265

Everywhere I look,
I see the evidence of the Divine Presence.

266

I have the wisdom to deal
with any situation that comes up.
I always keep the focus
on my power to succeed.

267

I am not envious of others' happiness.
I am happy for them and their happiness
is the mirror of mine.

268

I feel positive,
this is how I cultivate good luck.

269

*Every day I nurture my spirit
with good relationships.*

270

*I acknowledge my efforts.
I have done my best,
even when I have failed.*

271

*Instead of complaining
about situations I do not like,
I either accept them or I do
something to avoid them.*

272

I can light up
the world around myself
with a simple smile on my face.
So I smile.

273

Beyond my limited ego,
there is an unlimited Uni-verse
of Love.

274

Even in my darkest moments,
I remember that I am always a blessing,
a gift for someone. I remember that my light
always shines.

275

I stop considering time as my enemy.
The speed of life is no longer my obsession.
I realize how wonderful my state of Being
is in the Here and Now.

276

I do not look for
vanishing drops of happiness.
I tap into the infinite source of happiness:
Awareness.

277

Through forgiveness,
I transform the poison of resentment
into the honey of compassion.

278

I am true and honest to myself.

279.

I graciously accept compliments.
I deserve all the compliments I receive.

280

I receive all the Love of the world,
because I give all my Love to the world.

281

Beyond the apparent imperfection,
I see the perfection of my world.

282

I accept hard times with confidence:
I have grown up and I have learned
more during my difficult times
than in easy times.

283

I forgive those who have hurt me
and I forget the pain that
I have received and given.
In my heart there is no place
for anger and resentment.

284

I gently bring my truth to others
from a loving place.

285

*Today I make a difference
in someone else's life,
today I make a difference in my life.*

286

*Forgiving myself is
the most important thing I can do
for my health and for my wealth.*

287

*I bless the people that I struggle against.
They are in my life to give me
the chance to deepen my awareness
and love.*

288

Today I take a holiday
from myself, my duties and my worries.
Today I step outside my daily routine
and I do the unexpected.

289

Joy is my birthright.
Abundance is my birthright.
Love is my birthright.

290

I embrace differences
and I appreciate the uniqueness
of everyone else.

291

When I encounter negativity or hostility,
I align myself with Unconditional Love.

292

I shape my life in ways that serve
humanity's awakening.

293

My belief is stronger than my fear:
I make my dreams happen.

294

I am grateful and I constantly attract
into my life more to be grateful for.

295

Love is the meaning of my Life.

296

I do not hide my wounds
under an outward mask of strength,
I accept and I show my weaknesses
with honesty, without fear of being judged
by others.

297

In everything I do, I Am Love.

298

I am not a winner, I am not a loser, I Am.

299

Happiness
does not belong to my destiny:
happiness is my free choice.
I choose happiness.

300

Whatever I have done
and whatever I have thought
about what I have done,
I am always the perfect
and beloved Child of God.

301

I am myself, so others can be themselves.

302

*I awaken
to the infinite possibilities
of the present moment.*

303

*I deserve
all the Love of the Uni-verse
and the Uni-verse deserves
all my Love.*

304

*I lift my energies up
and miraculous synchronicities
happen in my life.*

305

I forgive myself,
I allow myself to be worthy
of love and happiness.

306

My mind is silent
and my heart is fearless.

307

I release any feelings of pride.
I turn my pride into humbleness.

308

I rely on Love.

309

*I always learn from my failures
and my failures become victories.*

310

*From now on everything will turn out
for the best in my life.*

311

*With the power of my inner light
I illuminate the darkness of this world.*

312

*I am an indivisible part of the Oneness.
I am a manifestation of the One Truth.*

313

I live without regrets, I live my passions.

314

The world is my mirror:
I smile and the world smiles back at me.

315

I allow myself to feel worthy
of the love I receive.

316

I have the courage to be myself
and I encourage others to be who they are.

317

The memory of my old suffering
brings me only new suffering,
now I choose to let go of
my painful memories.

318

I am grateful for everything
that has ever occurred
to bring me to the present moment.

319

Consciously using
the power of my Divine Nature,
I decree the end of my suffering
and the beginning of my new joyful life.

320

I release my resentment.
I bring peace to my difficult relationships.

321

I align every emotion, thought and action
with the purpose of my soul.

322

I open my heart,
I have so much love to share.

323

I am no better nor less than others.
I am unique.

324

*The faults
that annoy me in others,
are those I do not want to see in myself.*

325

*In every moment, all my loved ones
are divinely protected.*

326

What I believe is what happens to me.

327

*I inspire others
to become better and brighter.*

328

I practice compassion,
this is how I heal my own
and others' sufferings.

329

I release all my feelings of guilt
and I stop punishing myself
through shame and failures.
I forgive myself.

330

Stillness of the mind is the experience
that ends all my questions.

331

*I release my need
to judge and criticize myself
for failures and weaknesses
that I believe I have.*

332

*Nobody has the power
to make me feel unhappy,
unless I give them that power.*

333

*I am the perfect child of God,
created by Love to love.*

334

I cannot change what I have done,
but I forgive myself for having done it.

335

I look at others as
if they already radiate
their Divine Potential.

336.

In true Unconditional Love,
I do not expect anyone to change,
because everyone is perfect
just the way they are.

337

*I am a powerful, magnificent
expression of Divine Love.*

338

*I do not react
when I am out of balance,
I do not hurt myself and others.
I wait until I can act with love.*

339

*My dreams are
the key to happiness,
I never give up on my dreams.*

340

*I give freely
without expectation
and the Universe gives back to me
in unpredictable ways.*

341

*When I want to improve
something in my life,
there is only one place to start:
within myself.*

342

*I stop my stressful search
for perfection, I am perfect
just the way I am.*

343

I learn something new every day,
I let go of something old every day.

344

I live, I love and I let it be.

345

I allow myself to feel happy
without feeling guilty.

346

I recognize and honor
the sacredness of every human being.

347

*In the stillness of my mind, I listen
to the compassionate voice of my heart.*

348

*Only I can change my world,
no one else can do it for me.*

349

*Even if
the truth makes me uncomfortable,
I always seek truth.*

350

*I value and unconditionally
love myself.*

351

The Divine is present
in every breath I take.

352

My highest fulfilment is
Unconditional Love in the Oneness.

353

There is no better place than here.
There is no better time than now.

354

I am never alone,
in the Oneness nothing is separated
and loneliness is just an illusion.

355

I overcome my ego,
I develop the spirit of surrender.

356

I look at the world with purity
through the eyes of a child.

357

I love and bless what I want to release.

358

I end all my personal dramas,
I unconditionally accept
what life brings me.

359

Life always flows and changes,
I accept that my life is a journey
into the unknown full of
wonderful surprises.

360

Everyone
I encounter in my life
is a divine instrument that teaches me
what I need to learn, when I am
ready to learn.

361

My wealth and the measure
of my success is in the amount of love
that I give and receive.

362

I recognize and honor God in others,
I recognize and honor God within myself.

363

Despite everything, I believe in joy.

364

I am aware of how
my words and actions affect others.
I express Love in every word and action.

365

I choose to be the real me,
the very best me that I can be.

Appendix

Other books by Human Angels

We Are Human Angels
Find out why this book can truly change your life.

Have you always suffered because of your sensitivity? Have you always had the feeling of being out of place here on earth? Have you, from the very beginning, believed to be born for a greater purpose even though you did not know until now which one it could be? Within this book you will find all of the answers to the most profound questions about who you are and the meaning of your presence here on earth. By reading this book you will learn how to manage your intense sensitivity as a Human Angel and how to make the best use of it in helping others. This book will help you to find your own mission here on earth and to fulfill your highest potential as a Human Angel. "The 7 Keys to overcome the ego" and "The 7 keys to live with the heart in service to the Oneness" are the titles of the two parts of this book. Fourteen chapters to change your life forever, to guide you, step by step, on your journey in overcoming the ego and suffering, until the fulfillment of your true nature as a Human Angel. Within the pages of this book, you will find out that what seemed to be a burden weighing heavily on your shoulders over the years, were simply your wings.

We are Human Angels, with its unique story, is the book phenomenon of the web. In a very short time after its publication and thanks to the word of mouth of the readers, this self published book has become successful to the point of climbing the charts and ranking the top places among the titles of famous spiritual authors.

What makes the story of this book truly extraordinary is that many readers of different nationalities, driven by the deep wish to share its message, spontaneously started to contact us offering to translate the book into their native languages. Professional translators, teachers, headmasters, university students, artists, and many other kinds of wonderful people, have all passionately and generously participated in the diffusion of the book's message.

We are Human Angels can now count on many different translations (and other translations are yet to come) and has become the benchmark for the steadily increasing community of Human Angels in the world.

We are Human Angels is available on all major online bookstores, in paperback and as an ebook.

365 Wisdom Pills
Your daily dose of Angelic Wisdom

365 Wisdom Pills is the perfect completion to *365 Mantras for today*. It contains 365 ready-to-take pills of wisdom that you can choose to use together or in alternation with the mantras. The healing process is sometimes long, sometimes painful. These pills of wisdom are another tool for your spiritual awakening. As human beings living in a hectic world, we do not always need to read long, overstuffed sentences full of redundant words and pieces of advice. What we need is something that is at the same time both simple yet profound. Just like these pills. Take one or two of these pills and you will instantly feel better. You will look at the world around you with new eyes.

365 Wisdom Pills is available is available on all major online bookstores, both in digital format (ebook) and in paperback.

About the Authors

You will not find our names as we have chosen to pen our books as Human Angels, a collective identity that heartily welcomes, embraces and transcends our individuality and belongs to all those who have chosen to live with Unconditional Love in the Oneness. We have written these books driven by the wish to share our healing journey, a trip through the illusions of the ego to our rebirth in the Oneness. We have transmuted our experiences into Awareness and Love with the help of powerful, channeled energies that have, increasingly, guided and enlightened the path of our journey.

As self-published authors, a kind review is a gift for us!

If this book has touched your heart and opened your mind, please write a review on the store from which you have purchased the book.

Being self-published authors means that we do not have a publishing house supporting and promoting our books. The best way to make this book more visible to potential readers is by word of mouth of readers as well as good reviews.

A review is a gift for us. The more the reviews, the greater the visibility of the book and the higher the number of people who will be interested in reading it. It might be your review that will sparkle someone else's interest in the book, helping them to transform their lives.

1000 Thanks from us and from all those who will be inspired by your words!

Would you like to be part of this project of love?

Like our two other books, *365 Mantras for today* has been generously and spontaneously translated by the readers into many languages. If you would like to translate *365 Mantras for today* into your native language, please contact us: earthangelshouse@gmail.com. To find out which are the languages in which the book has already been translated, please visit our website.

Contacts

Website:
www.wearehumanangels.com
Email:
earthangelshouse@gmail.com
Facebook Page:
We Are Human Angels
Facebook Group:
Connecting Human Angels
Twitter:
@HUMAN_ANGELS
Hashtag:
#humanangel

Contents

Made in the USA
Lexington, KY
06 June 2016